Specific Skill Series

Following Directions

Richard A. Boning

Fifth Edition

SRA/McGraw-Hill
Columbus, Ohio

To the Teacher

PURPOSE:
FOLLOWING DIRECTIONS is designed to develop skill in reading, understanding, and following instructions and directions. Proficiency in this basic skill is essential for success in every school subject and in nonacademic activities as well.

FOR WHOM:
The skill of FOLLOWING DIRECTIONS is developed through a series of books spanning ten levels (Picture, Preparatory, A, B, C, D, E, F, G, H). The Picture Level is for pupils who have not acquired a basic sight vocabulary. The Preparatory Level is for pupils who have a basic sight vocabulary but are not yet ready for the first-grade-level book. Books A through H are appropriate for pupils who can read on levels one through eight, respectively. **The use of the *Specific Skill Series Placement Test* is recommended to determine the appropriate level.**

THE NEW EDITION:
The fifth edition of the *Specific Skill Series* maintains the quality and focus that has distinguished this program for more than 25 years. A key element central to the program's success has been the unique nature of the reading selections. Nonfiction pieces about current topics have been designed to stimulate the interest of students, motivating them to use the comprehension strategies they have learned to further their reading. To keep this important aspect of the program intact, a percentage of the reading selections have been replaced in order to ensure the continued relevance of the subject material.

In addition, a significant percentage of the artwork in the program has been replaced to give the books a contemporary look. The cover photographs are designed to appeal to readers of all ages.

SESSIONS:
Short practice sessions are the most effective. It is desirable to have a practice session every day or every other day, using a few units each session.

SCORING:
Pupils should record their answers on the reproducible worksheets. The worksheets make scoring easier and provide uniform records of the pupils' work. Using worksheets also avoids consuming the exercise books.

It is important for pupils to know how well they are doing. For this reason, units should be scored as soon as they have been completed. Then a discussion can be held in which pupils justify their choices. (The Integrated Language Activities, many of which are open-ended, do not lend themselves to an objective score; thus there are no answer keys for these pages.)

GENERAL INFORMATION ON *FOLLOWING DIRECTIONS*:

FOLLOWING DIRECTIONS focuses attention on four types of directions. The *testing and drilling* directions are like those in most textbooks and workbooks. Mastery of this type, so vital to school success, is stressed throughout FOLLOWING DIRECTIONS. The second type of direction is found in science books and involves *experimenting*. Such material requires the reader to find an answer to a problem or provides the reader with an example of practical application of a principle.

The third type of direction, *assembling*, deals with parts or ingredients and the order and way in which they are put together. Here the purpose is to make or create, rather than to solve a problem or demonstrate a principle.

Directions which tell how to do something are *performing* directions. They accent the steps in learning to do something new. The focus is on the performance rather than on the product.

SUGGESTED STEPS:

On levels A-H, pupils read the information above the first line. Then they answer the questions *below* this line. (Pupils are *not* to respond in writing to information *above* the first line; they are only to study it. Pupils should not write or mark anything in this book.) On the Picture Level, pupils tell if a picture correctly follows the directions. On the Preparatory Level, pupils tell which picture out of two correctly follows the directions.

Additional information on using FOLLOWING DIRECTIONS with pupils will be found in the **Specific Skill Series Teacher's Manual**.

RELATED MATERIALS:

Specific Skill Series Placement Tests, which enable the teacher to place pupils at their appropriate levels in each skill, are available for the Elementary (Pre-1–6) and Midway (4–8) grade levels.

About This Book

Following directions is like trying to find your way in a strange place by using a road map. If you follow the directions correctly, you will get where you want to go. If you do not understand the directions, or if you make mistakes in following them, you will become lost.

Reading directions is different from reading a story or an article. When you read directions, you should read slowly and carefully. You should reread anything you do not understand and find out the meanings of any special terms that are used. When you are following directions, you need to follow them in the right order. Direction words, such as *top*, *bottom*, *right*, and *left*, are especially important.

In this book, you will read four different kinds of directions. You will read directions that are like the directions you often find on tests and in workbooks. You will read directions that tell you how to conduct experiments and directions for putting things together. You will also read directions for doing things, such as playing a game.

After you read each set of directions, you will answer questions about the directions. One question is about the purpose of the directions. Others are about details in the directions. Read each set of directions carefully so that you can answer the questions about them.

DIRECTIONS: You can make your own liquid soap. Use a bar of soap made from natural materials. Grate the soap into a saucepan with a vegetable grater. Cover the gratings with water. Simmer the mixture on low heat for two hours. Remove the melted soap from the stove and let it cool. Pour it into a storage container. Use your homemade soap to wash dishes.

1. The directions tell you how to—
   - **(A) make a bar of soap**
   - **(C) make liquid soap**
   - **(B) wash dishes in the dishwasher**
   - **(D) grate vegetables**

2. Grate a bar of soap into a—
   - **(A) dishwasher**
   - **(C) saucepan**
   - **(B) plastic container**
   - **(D) paper bag**

3. Cover the soap with water and—
   - **(A) heat it in the oven**
   - **(C) simmer it for two hours**
   - **(B) let it stand in the sun**
   - **(D) pour it into a container**

4. Remove the melted soap from the stove and—
   - **(A) let it harden**
   - **(C) let it cool**
   - **(B) use it immediately**
   - **(D) put it into the refrigerator**

UNIT 2

DIRECTIONS: For a tailored, businesslike look in curtains, buy or make straight, lined panels to hang over window blinds. Measure the length of the panels from the exact top of the window to the sill, so no material will hang over. The curtains must be wide enough so they can be folded back and pinned to look like openings in a tent. The material for the curtains should fit in with the room. The coloring should more or less match the wall covering. Such curtains are sometimes called campaign curtains.

1. These directions show you how to—
   - **(A) make window blinds**
   - **(B) sew wall coverings**
   - **(C) line a tent**
   - **(D) make tailored curtains**

2. The curtains are folded back and—
   - **(A) cut**
   - **(B) washed**
   - **(C) painted**
   - **(D) pinned**

3. The wall covering should blend with or match the—
   - **(A) plants**
   - **(B) sidewalk**
   - **(C) shingles**
   - **(D) curtains**

4. When folded back to look like openings in a tent, these hangings are sometimes called—
   - **(A) campaign curtains**
   - **(B) balloon drapes**
   - **(C) cafe curtains**
   - **(D) swags**

DIRECTIONS: Open a 9-ounce can of tuna. Spoon half of the contents into a mixing bowl. Then add some chopped celery and onions and mix with mayonnaise or salad dressing. Cut the sides off two slices of pita bread so that each piece has an open pocket. Toast the pita bread pockets until they are warm but not brown. Fill the pita pockets with the tuna mixture. Eat one and serve one to a friend. Soon the whole neighborhood will come knocking at your door!

1. From this article you learn how to—
   - (A) chop celery
   - (B) make pita pockets
   - (C) have a friend to lunch
   - (D) make tuna-pita bread sandwiches

2. After mixing the tuna and chopped celery,—
   - (A) toast the pita bread
   - (B) add mayonnaise
   - (C) open the tuna
   - (D) spoon the tuna into a bowl

3. Before you toast the pita bread,—
   - (A) cut the sides to make pockets
   - (B) spoon out the tuna
   - (C) cut up celery and onions
   - (D) serve one sandwich to a friend

4. Before you fill the pockets with the tuna mixture,—
   - (A) add mayonnaise
   - (B) lightly toast the pita bread
   - (C) add more tuna
   - (D) spoon out half the tuna

UNIT 4

DIRECTIONS: Gather the reins in your left hand. Put your left hand on the horse's neck. Then take your right foot out of the stirrup. Swing your right leg upward and backward over the horse's back without touching it. Put your right hand on the rear of the saddle and your right forearm on the saddle seat. Lean on the right forearm until you release your left foot from the stirrup. Be sure it is free and clear. Now drop to the ground.

1. These directions show you how to—
    (A) make a horse jump
    (B) get on a horse
    (C) dismount from a horse
    (D) stop a horse

2. Don't drop to the ground until—
    (A) your left foot is free
    (B) you are told
    (C) the horse says, "Go ahead"
    (D) you are one foot above it

3. Your right leg should—
    (A) touch the horse's back
    (B) touch the horse's tail
    (C) not touch the horse's back
    (D) swing forward

4. Until your left foot is out of the stirrup,—
    (A) lean on the horse's head
    (B) lean on the horse's neck
    (C) lean on your right forearm
    (D) lean on the left forearm

DIRECTIONS: There is a correct way to lift things from the floor. First, bend your knees and squat down. Keep your back straight. Don't bend over from the waist as you attempt to pick up a heavy object. This puts the whole strain on your lower-back muscles. Try to get as close to the object as you can. To do this you may have to spread your knees or lower one knee. Keep the object close to your body. Use your leg muscles to rise.

1. These directions show you how to—
   - (A) lift things from the floor
   - (B) take things down from a shelf
   - (C) push things around
   - (D) strengthen your muscles

2. It is important to—
   - (A) use your arm muscles
   - (B) strain your back muscles
   - (C) use your shoulder muscles
   - (D) keep close to the object

3. Remember to keep—
   - (A) your back straight
   - (B) your legs straight
   - (C) far from the object
   - (D) your back bent

4. You may have to—
   - (A) bend from your waist
   - (B) bend from your shoulders
   - (C) bend backwards
   - (D) lower one knee

UNIT 6

DIRECTIONS: As you spring up, try to get your hips higher than your head. Wait until you reach your highest point before you start the jackknife. Keep your legs straight with toes pointing down to the water. Bend at the hips. Reach down with outstretched arms to touch your pointed toes. Hold this jackknife position a short while. Then throw your legs back. This will allow you to enter the water with your body straight.

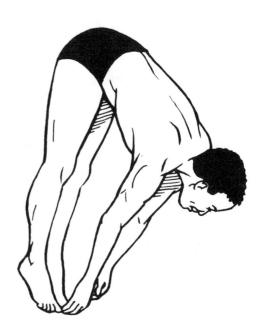

1. These directions show you how to—
   - (A) touch your toes
   - (C) carve with a jackknife
   - (B) do one kind of dive
   - (D) swim

2. Remember to—
   - (A) keep your legs bent
   - (C) bend your arms
   - (B) bend at the knees
   - (D) keep your legs straight

3. To straighten out, throw your—
   - (A) legs forward
   - (C) arms forward
   - (B) legs backward
   - (D) arms backward

4. You start the jackknife—
   - (A) right away
   - (C) just before you enter the water
   - (B) as you come down
   - (D) just as you reach your highest point

DIRECTIONS: If you are having trouble with a clogged drain, you may be able to save money by following these directions. Before calling a plumber or buying an expensive drain cleaner, take some baking soda and vinegar from your kitchen supplies. Put a handful of baking soda down the clogged drain. Add one-half cup of vinegar. Cover the drain tightly for about a minute. You may be pleased to find out that the drain works again.

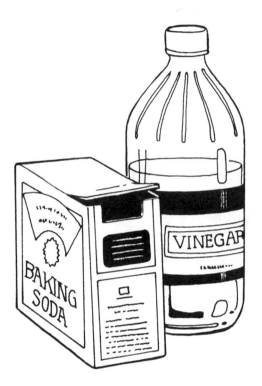

1. These directions teach you a simple way to fix a—
   - (A) leaky pipe
   - (B) running faucet
   - (C) clogged drain
   - (D) broken sink

2. The supplies you need are—
   - (A) soda and flavoring
   - (B) vinegar and baking soda
   - (C) oil and vinegar
   - (D) baking powder and salt

3. The vinegar is poured down the drain after the—
   - (A) salt
   - (B) water
   - (C) drain cleaner
   - (D) baking soda

4. Cover the drain tightly for—
   - (A) an hour
   - (B) five minutes
   - (C) one second
   - (D) a minute

DIRECTIONS: If you should get lost, build signal fires. First, choose the most open spot that you can find. Get away from tall trees, as they break up or hide smoke columns. Build three fires, about ten feet apart, if you have enough fuel. Smoke from one fire isn't unusual enough to attract attention! Once you are sure that the fire is going well, pile on rotten wood, green grass, leaves, or limbs. Then you will have a dark, dense smoke that can be seen from a great distance.

1. The purpose of the directions is to teach you to—
   (A) keep warm
   (B) make a cooking fire
   (C) build signal fires
   (D) put out fires

2. You should build the fires—
   (A) in the woods
   (B) close to home
   (C) in a clearing
   (D) to trick people

3. To get a lot of smoke, use—
   (A) coal
   (B) green grass
   (C) oil
   (D) oak

4. Remember to build—
   (A) just one fire
   (B) three fires
   (C) fires four feet apart
   (D) fires about twenty-five feet apart

DIRECTIONS: Keep your body perfectly flat and well extended. Keep your feet and toes pointed downward. Your feet should be limp, your legs straight, and your knees relaxed. Don't bend your knees very much. Make the power come from your hips. Kick one leg and then the other, with little or no splashing. Only the heel or the back half of your foot should break water. Your kick should not be fast, just easy and steady.

1. These directions teach you how to—
   - (A) move your arms
   - (B) rescue others
   - (C) dive
   - (D) kick

2. Remember to—
   - (A) splash
   - (B) stay perfectly flat
   - (C) bend at the waist
   - (D) kick very fast

3. The power comes from your—
   - (A) arms
   - (B) feet
   - (C) hips
   - (D) knees

4. Your feet and toes should—
   - (A) be tense
   - (B) point downward
   - (C) point in and up
   - (D) not move

DIRECTIONS: Stand on the mat with your legs a full step apart and your arms horizontal and out to the sides. Start your cartwheel by shifting your weight sideward to your left foot, and lift your right foot off the ground. Bend sideways from the waist. As you put your left hand on the mat, raise your right leg in a sideward and upward swing. Don't bend your knees or elbows. For a split second you will be upside down with your legs wide apart. Continue your sideward motion. Land on your right foot in position to do another cartwheel.

1. This article was written to show you how to do a—
   (A) **backward roll**
   (B) **cartwheel**
   (C) **sit-up**
   (D) **forward roll**

2. When you put your left hand on the mat,—
   (A) **bend your knees**
   (B) **lower your right hand**
   (C) **raise your left leg**
   (D) **raise your right leg**

3. Your legs should be—
   (A) **bent**
   (B) **kept together**
   (C) **straight**
   (D) **on the mat always**

4. Remember to bend—
   (A) **your arms**
   (B) **your knees**
   (C) **sideways**
   (D) **forward**

DIRECTIONS: Stand in the center of the canoe. Make sure it's steady. Keep your back bent and your weight low. Grasp both sides of the canoe with your hands. Keep your weight on both hands and jump or vault sideways. Separate your legs just as they enter the water. Close your legs quickly so that you won't go completely under. As you enter the water, keep one hand on the near side of the canoe so that it won't float away.

1. The directions explain how to—
   (A) **enter a boat**   (B) **paddle a canoe**
   (C) **swim**   (D) **vault from a canoe**

2. At first, your hands should be—
   (A) **on your hips**   (B) **on the sides**
   (C) **straight up**   (D) **wet**

3. You won't go completely under if you—
   (A) **are very light**   (B) **straighten up**
   (C) **close your legs**   (D) **jump upward**

4. You must remember to—
   (A) **let go of the canoe**   (B) **swim for your life**
   (C) **keep your weight low**   (D) **yell for help**

DIRECTIONS: Position yourself near the center of the canoe but more toward the stern, or back. Rest back on your heels with your knees and legs on the bottom. If the wind is strong, move more toward the bow. Hold your upper hand over the grip of the paddle. Wrap your lower hand around the shaft of the paddle, about three or four inches above the blade. Keep your lower arm straight. Start your stroke with your upper hand in front of your shoulder. Extend your lower arm to its full length. Then stroke. Each time the paddle comes out of the water, keep its blade parallel to the water. Then stroke again. This is called "feathering" and is part of learning to paddle a canoe.

1. This article was written to show you how to—
   (A) handle a boat
   (B) rescue swimmers
   (C) paddle a canoe
   (D) move against the current

2. After you position yourself behind the center of the canoe,—
   (A) lean forward
   (B) rest back on your heels
   (C) sit on the seat
   (D) begin to paddle

3. If the head wind is strong,—
   (A) move forward
   (B) crouch lower
   (C) move to the rear
   (D) turn sideways

4. Your lower hand should be above the—
   (A) blade
   (B) shaft
   (C) grip
   (D) shoulder

A. Exercising Your Skill

Directions give you steps to follow. When you follow directions, read them carefully, and follow the steps in the right order.

HOMEMADE PASTA

What you need: 3 cups flour, 4 eggs, rolling pin, knife, large pot

What you do:

1. Put the flour in a heap on a clean tabletop. Make a well in the middle of the heap, and break the eggs into it. Mix them into the flour. Keep working the mixture until it is rubbery.
2. Sprinkle flour on the table. Divide the dough into three balls, and roll out each ball into thin sheets.
3. Let the dough sheets dry for ten minutes. Then sprinkle some flour on them and roll them up.
4. Slice each roll into strips as wide as you want your noodles to be. Boil the pasta in a large pot of water for two or three minutes.

Answer these questions about the directions.

- Why are materials listed at the beginning?
- Why are the steps arranged as they are?
- How can you tell in what order to follow the steps?

B. Expanding Your Skill

With your classmates, talk about how pasta is made. Answer these questions.

- What things do you need to make pasta?
- What do you do first?
- What other things do you do?
- What things might happen if you did not follow the steps in the right order?

C. Exploring Language

Following directions is important in preparing and making something, whether it's food, clothing, models, or toys. Work with a small group of classmates. Together, make a list of materials needed to make paper-bag masks. To help you think of things, ask yourselves these questions:

- What size should the bags be?
- Where would they come from?
- What is needed for drawing, coloring, cutting, and pasting?
- What extra materials might be needed for decorations or parts like "hair" or "noses"?

After the materials are gathered, each member of the group should write his or her own set of clear, easy-to-follow directions for how to make a mask that looks _____ . (For example: your directions could say *scary*, *ugly*, *funny*, or *beautiful*; or *like a clown, rabbit, space creature*, or *monster*.) Be sure the steps are in the right order. Give your directions to a classmate in your group to follow. Then follow the directions you are given. When the masks are finished, have fun wearing them.

D. Expressing Yourself

Choose one of these activities.

1. Find a recipe that tells how to make one of your favorite foods. Bring the recipe to class, and explain how to make the food.

2. Make up a set of directions for cooking a particular food or for making a toy such as a puppet or kite. Read the directions to your classmates—but don't tell them the name of the food or toy. Ask them to guess what the directions will make.

3. Find directions for a game you have never played before. With a classmate, read the directions carefully and play the game. Then teach another classmate how to play the game. Give clear directions.

DIRECTIONS: Swimming is more fun when you keep water safety in mind. First, learn how to swim from a parent or in a water safety course. Swim only in a pool or lake where there is a lifeguard on duty. Never swim in an unguarded lake or pond. Swim with a buddy whenever possible. Keep your eye on him or her and have your buddy do the same for you. When learning to swim, stay in the shallow part of the pool or lake.

1. The article was written to teach you how to—
   (A) swim and dive   **(B) become a lifeguard**
   (C) choose a swimming buddy   **(D) be safe in the water**

2. When you swim in a pool or lake, make sure there is a—
   (A) deep end   **(B) diving board**
   (C) ladder   **(D) lifeguard**

3. Always keep your eye on your—
   (A) parents   **(B) lifeguard**
   (C) swimming teacher   **(D) buddy**

4. If you are just learning to swim,—
   (A) stay out of the water   **(B) talk to the lifeguard**
   (C) dive in the shallow end   **(D) stay in the shallow end**

DIRECTIONS: Have someone watch you. Take a deep breath. Now you are ready to try a headfirst surface dive. Bend from the hips, head first. Make sure that the upper part of your body is well underwater. Then throw your legs back and straight up into the air. This will help propel your body downward. Arch your back. Take one powerful stroke with both arms, and bring your arms along your sides to prevent drag. Don't begin kicking until your feet are completely under water.

1. The directions show you how to make a—
   - **(A) swan dive**
   - **(C) running dive**
   - **(B) surface dive**
   - **(D) back dive**

2. Remember to—
   - **(A) throw your legs downward**
   - **(C) bend from the knee**
   - **(B) bend from the hips**
   - **(D) enter feet first**

3. After you make a stroke, keep your arms—
   - **(A) out of the water**
   - **(C) by your sides**
   - **(B) straight ahead**
   - **(D) sticking out sideways**

4. You must—
   - **(A) be by yourself**
   - **(C) enter headfirst**
   - **(B) take half a breath**
   - **(D) keep your back perfectly straight**

DIRECTIONS: Fill the cracks with putty. Then smooth them with fine sandpaper. Unscrew the doorknob and other hardware. First, apply paint to the panel with horizontal strokes. Then finish with light vertical strokes. Begin with the molded edges on the center panel (1). Then paint that panel. Next, paint panels (2) and (3) in the same way. Paint hinge edge (4) from the top down. Paint crossboards (5), (6), and (7). Paint vertical boards (8) and (9) last.

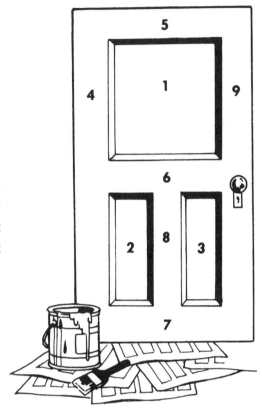

1. These directions tell you how to—
   - (A) **paint a door**
   - (B) **prepare a door for painting**
   - (C) **paint more neatly**
   - (D) **paint panels on walls**

2. Before you use sandpaper,—
   - (A) **fill the cracks with putty**
   - (B) **remove the hardware**
   - (C) **take off the doorknob**
   - (D) **paint with horizontal strokes**

3. Paint the hinge edge before you paint the—
   - (A) **center panel**
   - (B) **hinges**
   - (C) **crossboards**
   - (D) **walls**

4. Before you paint the molded edges on the center panel,—
   - (A) **fill the cracks with putty**
   - (B) **paint the crossboards**
   - (C) **remove the hardware**
   - (D) **paint the center panel**

UNIT 16

DIRECTIONS: Tell the class that you are about to perform an unusual experiment. Get two thermometers. Cover one with a white cloth. Then cover the other with a black cloth. Set both thermometers in the sun. Ask the class which cloth will do a better job of reflecting the heat rays. Let the class vote. In thirty minutes remove the cloth from each thermometer. The thermometers will give you the answer.

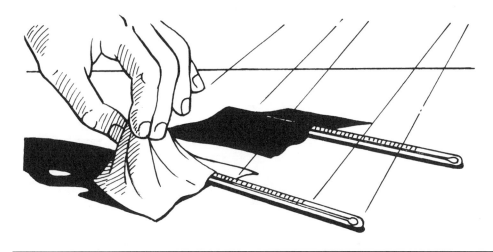

1. This experiment shows how—
   - **(A) to select a thermometer**
   - **(B) to use a thermometer**
   - **(C) to purchase a thermometer**
   - **(D) different colors reflect heat**

2. After you cover the two thermometers,—
   - **(A) get the class to vote**
   - **(B) set them in the sun**
   - **(C) tell the class about the experiment**
   - **(D) soak the cloths in water**

3. This article shows you how to—
   - **(A) teach proper heating**
   - **(B) read a thermometer**
   - **(C) conduct group experiments**
   - **(D) demonstrate which color absorbs heat more readily**

4. After you remove the cloths,—
   - **(A) ask the class to vote**
   - **(B) look at the thermometers**
   - **(C) leave the thermometers in the sun for half an hour**
   - **(D) tell the class about the experiment**

DIRECTIONS: Lie on the floor, face down. Keep your legs together. Put your hands on the floor beside your shoulders. Point your fingers straight ahead. Now straighten your arms to push your body off the floor. Your weight should be on your hands and toes. Don't let your stomach sag. Don't arch your back. Keep your body straight. Lower your body until your chest barely touches the floor. Push yourself right up again without any delay. Keep repeating the exercise.

1. These directions show you how to do—
    (A) sit-ups   (B) toe touches
    (C) push-ups   (D) knee bends

2. It's important to—
    (A) lift your knees   (B) turn your head
    (C) curl up   (D) keep your body straight

3. When you lower yourself,—
    (A) push up again   (B) touch with your whole body
    (C) rest for a spell   (D) touch with your knees

4. Your weight should be carried by your—
    (A) arms   (B) hands and toes
    (C) shoulders   (D) legs

DIRECTIONS: Put out the fire by sprinkling it with water. Splash it on with your hand. Do not pour it on. A solid stream of water sometimes leaves part of a fire untouched. Stir the wet embers with a stick. Then sprinkle again, thoroughly. Before you leave the scene, check again by putting your hand right on the ashes. After the wet ashes have cooled off, bury them. If no water is available, use plain sand or soil to put out the fire.

1. The purpose of this article is to show you how to—
   (A) start a fire
   (B) put out a fire
   (C) prevent prairie fires
   (D) avoid burns

2. If water is not available, you should smother the fire with—
   (A) dirt
   (B) leaves
   (C) branches
   (D) a blanket

3. Do not pour a steady stream of water on the fire because this—
   (A) may leave some hot ashes untouched
   (B) creates too much steam
   (C) makes the flames grow
   (D) creates sparks

4. After you first sprinkle water on the fire,—
   (A) touch it
   (B) bury it with soil
   (C) sprinkle it again
   (D) stir the wet ashes

DIRECTIONS: You must be skating fast to use the so-called "hockey stop." Start gliding with your feet together. Don't move your shoulders. Now make a sudden turn of your body, from below your shoulders. Your feet, legs, and hips must quickly turn at an angle away from the direction in which you've been traveling. Keep both feet flat on the ice and parallel. Use both as brakes. Your arms must be extended. Lean away from the stop as you slow down. Straighten up when you come to a full stop.

1. These directions tell you how to—
   - (A) make a snowplow stop
   - (B) get a fast start
   - (C) make a hockey stop
   - (D) skate backward

2. Your feet should—
   - (A) not scrape the ice
   - (B) be facing in different directions
   - (C) be used as brakes
   - (D) not be used as brakes

3. As you slow down,—
   - (A) stand straight
   - (B) take a bow
   - (C) lean forward
   - (D) lean away from the stop

4. Your arms must—
   - (A) be by your sides
   - (B) be folded
   - (C) act as brakes
   - (D) be extended

DIRECTIONS: First, magnetize a needle. Do this by stroking the length of the needle with a bar magnet. Stroke from the eye to the point of the needle. Next, shove the needle through a cork. Then place the cork in a glass of water. Allow the cork to float freely in the water. (Make certain that no other magnet or object made of iron is near. Otherwise, the needle will be pulled in that direction.) Now the end of the needle containing the eye should be pointing north.

1. From this story, you learn how to—
   - (A) **avoid getting lost**
   - (B) **make a compass**
   - (C) **magnetize water**
   - (D) **read a compass**

2. Stroke the needle—
   - (A) **with a magnet**
   - (B) **through the cork**
   - (C) **toward the center**
   - (D) **toward the eye**

3. If a magnet or an iron object is nearby,—
   - (A) **the cork will sink**
   - (B) **the needle will float**
   - (C) **the needle will point straight up**
   - (D) **the compass will not be accurate**

4. The eye of the needle should point—
   - (A) **home**
   - (B) **north**
   - (C) **up**
   - (D) **down**

DIRECTIONS: Look up the new word in a dictionary. Read its definition. Next, try to sound out the word, using the pronunciation guide in the dictionary. Usually this is found at the top or bottom of each page. Look back at the paragraph where you found the new word used. Do you understand the author's meaning more clearly? Think of a sentence in which the word might be used. Write the word on a card. Beside the word write the definition. Build a collection of these cards. Review them frequently.

alphabet [Greek *o mikron,* "small o" : *o* + *mikron,* neuter of *mikros,* small (see *smē-* in Appendix*).]

om·i·nous (ŏm'ə-nəs) *adj.* **1.** Being or pertaining to an evil omen; portentous; foreboding: "*The Mountain standing ominous and* ... *had looked taller than it was.*" (J.R.R. Tolkien). **2.** ... ; threatening: "*The growl outside turned more om-inous* ... mas Pynchon). [Latin *ōminōsus,* from *ōmen* (stem *ōmin-* ...] —**om'i·nous·ly** *adv.* —**om'i·nous·ness** *n.*

o·mis· ... mis'ə-bəl) *adj.* Capable of or fit for omission. [From ... past participle *omissus-*), OMIT.]

o·mis· ... act or an instance of omitting: "We ... *this curious omission we are*

1. This article was written to show you how to—
   (A) improve your vocabulary   (B) get better grades
   (C) be a better English student   (D) impress your friends

2. After you see a new word, you should first—
   (A) write it down   (B) sound it out
   (C) use it   (D) look it up in a dictionary

3. Before you write down the word on a card,—
   (A) sound it out   (B) look up the definition
   (C) use it in a sentence   (D) review your cards

4. After you look up the definition, you should—
   (A) review your card   (B) use it in a sentence
   (C) sound out the word   (D) write it down

DIRECTIONS: If the victim's skin is flushed, hot, and dry; if the pulse is rapid and the temperature is 100° or more; if there has been lengthy exposure to the sun, the person may be suffering with sunstroke. Call the doctor immediately. Bring the victim indoors. Loosen the clothing. When in a prone position, cool the body by sponging with cold water or cold compresses. If conscious, give sips of cold salt water to drink. Use one-half teaspoon of salt per glass of water.

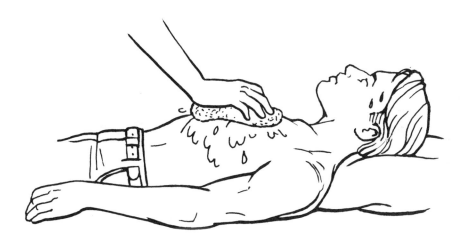

1. This article shows you how to provide help for—
   - **(A) sunburn**
   - **(C) a sunstroke victim**
   - **(B) a nosebleed**
   - **(D) a headache**

2. The cold drinking water should have—
   - **(A) salt in it**
   - **(C) lemon juice in it**
   - **(B) sugar in it**
   - **(D) nothing in it**

3. Before you get help, the skin of the victim will be—
   - **(A) tanned**
   - **(C) wet**
   - **(B) cool**
   - **(D) hot and dry**

4. The first thing you should do is—
   - **(A) make the victim run**
   - **(C) fan the victim**
   - **(B) cover the victim with blankets**
   - **(D) call the doctor**

DIRECTIONS: To make a carrot-top garden, you will need three or four carrots, a small kitchen knife, a shallow, flat-bottomed dish about four inches in diameter, and a handful of small pebbles. Use the knife to cut the tops off the carrots, leaving about an inch of carrot at each top. (Keep the remaining parts of the carrots to eat later.) Place the pebbles in the dish. Then place the carrot tops on the pebbles, cut-side down. Add a little water, just to the top of the pebbles. Place the dish in a sunny spot. Keep the pebbles moist. In about a week, the carrot tops will begin to sprout. Then the sprouts will grow into lacy green plants.

1. This article tells you how to—
   (A) peel a carrot
   (B) make carrot sticks
   (C) slice a carrot
   (D) make a carrot-top garden

2. To cut off the tops, use a—
   (A) potato peeler
   (B) tablespoon
   (C) scissors
   (D) kitchen knife

3. You will place the carrot tops on—
   (A) soil
   (B) a knife
   (C) some lettuce
   (D) pebbles

4. The carrot tops will sprout in about a—
   (A) month
   (B) week
   (C) year
   (D) day

UNIT 24

DIRECTIONS: You might enjoy having a guinea pig for a pet. This animal is easy to care for and has a playful, affectionate nature. You will need these supplies: a large aquarium (the twenty-gallon size) or a wire-sided cage about two feet long, pine or cedar chips, guinea pig food, and a water bottle. To care for your guinea pig, cover the bottom of the guinea pig's "home" with the wood chips. Keep a dish full of food in one corner. (It's important to use *guinea pig* food, not dry cat food or rabbit pellets, as it contains the extra vitamin C that guinea pigs require.) Hang the water bottle on one side and keep it filled with fresh water. The wood chips should be replaced about every four or five days. Have fun watching and playing with your guinea pig!

1. The purpose of this article is to show you—
   - (A) what a guinea pig eats
   - (B) why a guinea pig is playful
   - (C) how to play with a guinea pig
   - (D) how to care for a guinea pig

2. In the bottom of the cage put—
   - (A) an aquarium
   - (B) food
   - (C) pine or cedar chips
   - (D) the water bottle

3. This animal should eat only—
   - (A) guinea pig food
   - (B) dry cat food
   - (C) rabbit pellets
   - (D) hamster food

4. Your pet guinea pig will be fun to—
   - (A) replace
   - (B) hunt for
   - (C) watch and play with
   - (D) supply with vitamins

A. Exercising Your Skill

Directions give you steps to follow. The steps should be followed in order. The steps may be numbered, or they may use words like *first, next, then,* and *finally.* Read the following directions for linking paper clips.

LINKING PAPER CLIPS

Challenge friends to join two paper clips together without touching or holding them. They won't be able to until you show them the secret.

First you will need a dollar bill (or a piece of paper the same size) and two paper clips. Next, fold the bill into three parts. Think of the three parts of the bill as A, B, and C. Then clip one paper clip to two layers of the bill, one from A and one from B. Next, clip the other clip to two layers of the bill, one from B and one from C. The two clips should not touch each other. After that, hold the ends of the bill—one hand on each end—without touching the clips. Finally, pull the ends of the bill in opposite directions. The paper clips will link as if by magic!

What words in the directions helped you know the order to follow? On your paper, list the words.

B. Expanding Your Skill

Talk with your classmates about the list of time-order words you wrote. Can you think of other words that the writer could have used? Work together to add more time-order words to the list.

C. Exploring Language

The directions below are out of order, and they do not use any time-order words. Rewrite the directions so that the steps are in the right order. Then add time-order words to help show the order of the steps to be followed.

MAGIC PAPER CLIP

Turn the box over so that no one will know about the magnet but you.

Tape a strong magnet inside a thin cardboard box, placing the magnet on one side near the bottom.

Tape the thread to a table or desk.

Carefully push the box away from the clip until the clip is hanging in midair!

Hold the clip against the box at the point where the magnet is hidden.

Tie a paper clip to a piece of thread.

D. Expressing Yourself

Choose one of these activities.

1. Gather the materials for doing one or both of the magic tricks on these pages. Follow the directions, and perform the tricks. Tell what you are doing as you perform.

2. Find a book of simple magic tricks in the library. Follow the directions and learn some of the tricks. Put on a short magic show for your classmates.

3. Make up a magic trick of your own. Write a set of directions for performing the trick. Be sure to list the materials needed and to write the steps in order. See whether a classmate can follow the directions and do the trick.

DIRECTIONS: Do you have a hose that leaks? If the leak is small, fix it yourself. Cover the hole with a heavy coat of black rubber cement. After the first coat sets, apply a second coat. Then wrap the area with friction tape. If the leak can't be repaired this way, cut out the bad section. Then insert a metal splicer into one end. Hammer down the prongs. Do the same with the other end of the hose. Now you have joined both ends together.

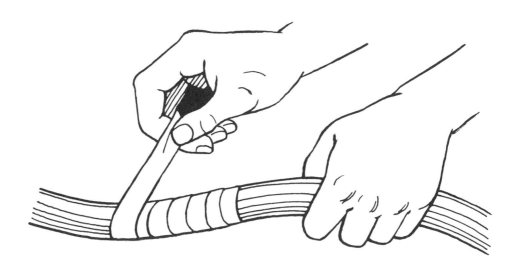

1. The purpose of this article is to show you how to—
   - (A) grow a better lawn
   - (B) repair a leaky hose
   - (C) use a hose
   - (D) become an expert

2. After the first coat of cement sets,—
   - (A) apply a second coat
   - (B) test the hose
   - (C) use a sprinkler
   - (D) cut off the end

3. Before you hammer down the prongs,—
   - (A) be sure the hose leaks
   - (B) pry them loose
   - (C) insert a metal splicer
   - (D) turn on the water

4. Before you put on friction tape,—
   - (A) try glue
   - (B) take the hose to a garage
   - (C) listen for escaping air
   - (D) apply two coats of cement

DIRECTIONS: Write the "magic number" 12345679. (Omit number 8.) Tell a friend to choose any number from 1 to 9. Your friend must tell you the number. Multiply that number by 9 in your head. Write the result under the magic number. Let's say, for example, that your friend chooses number 4. Multiply it by 9 and put 36 below the 12345679. Then ask your friend to multiply 12345679 by 36. The answer will be a surprise. It will consist only of 4's, the number originally chosen by your friend. No matter what number your friend chooses, the final answer after multiplying will always contain only that number.

12345679

1. These directions teach you—
   (A) how to count
   (C) a multiplication trick
   (B) a division trick
   (D) how to add

2. The "magic number" omits—
   (A) number 2
   (C) number 3
   (B) number 5
   (D) number 8

3. Your friend's number should always be—
   (A) multiplied by 9
   (C) multiplied by 6
   (B) multiplied by 5
   (D) multiplied by 3

4. The numbers in the answer will all be the same as—
   (A) your friend's number
   (C) number 3
   (B) number 7
   (D) number 10

DIRECTIONS: The swan dive is an up-and-out, slow, gliding kind of a dive. Just after you reach the high point, take a birdlike position. Put your arms out sideways with the palms down. Arch your back slightly and tilt your head back. Stay in this position for almost the whole dive. A split second before you enter the water, bring your arms forward of your head. Above all, keep your legs straight, closed, and rigid.

1. The purpose of the directions is to teach you—
   (A) to enter water   **(B) how to swim**
   (C) to swan dive   **(D) to be a bird**

2. Just before you enter the water, bring your arms—
   (A) forward   **(B) sideward**
   (C) backward   **(D) in and out**

3. Your legs must be—
   (A) bent   **(B) loose**
   (C) straight   **(D) wide apart**

4. Throughout most of the dive, your arms should be—
   (A) out sideways   **(B) bent**
   (C) arched   **(D) forward**

DIRECTIONS: Move toward the ground ball, especially if there is someone on base. As the ball comes near, stop. Bend low. Get down on one knee to be sure that the ball won't go through your legs. Make sure your glove is touching the ground. Scoop up the ball in your glove. Trap it in the glove with your right hand. In one swift, flowing motion throw it to the base toward which the runner is heading. Don't waste time in getting the ball away.

1. This article tells you how to—
   - (A) throw a ball
   - (B) catch a fly ball
   - (C) catch a ground ball
   - (D) bat

2. Make sure that your glove—
   - (A) touches the ground
   - (B) is held high
   - (C) is big enough
   - (D) is well padded

3. As the ball comes near,—
   - (A) stand up straight
   - (B) stop
   - (C) look at the batter
   - (D) keep running

4. If someone is on base, you should definitely—
   - (A) stand still
   - (B) run backward
   - (C) move toward the ball
   - (D) forget about the runner

DIRECTIONS: Here is how to baffle some friends. Ask one of them to volunteer to write down his or her house number. The friend is not to show the number to you. The friend will double the house number and add 5. Then the volunteer will multiply the total by 50. The friend's own age plus the number of days in a year (365) are added next. From this total the friend will subtract 615. Now the volunteer has the final figure. The two digits on the right give you the friend's age. The number preceding them is the friend's house number.

1. The purpose of this article is to show you how to—
   (A) find your way home
   (B) get on television
   (C) play the numbers game
   (D) find your way in a strange city

2. This trick will not work if—
   (A) the house number has only one digit
   (B) your friend shows you the figures
   (C) the volunteer is untruthful
   (D) one moves to a new house

3. Right after the volunteer multiplies by 50,—
   (A) 615 is subtracted
   (B) the results are totaled
   (C) the volunteer's own age is added
   (D) the number of days in a year is added

4. Right before subtracting 615, the friend's—
   (A) address is subtracted
   (B) house number is doubled
   (C) telephone number is multiplied
   (D) age and the days in a year are added

DIRECTIONS: Find a flowering plant in your yard or in a vacant lot. Cut a specimen, including a stem, some leaves, and a flower. At home, wash the dirt off the specimen. Blot it with paper towels and arrange it with all parts showing on an open sheet of newspaper. Fold the newspaper over and put it between two large sheets of blotting paper. Then place it between heavy books in a warm, dry room for several days. When the specimen is dry, tape it to a large sheet of thick paper. Write the plant's name and location at the bottom.

1. This article tells you how to—
   - **(A) find plants**
   - **(C) preserve plants**
   - **(B) identify plants**
   - **(D) photograph plants**

2. After washing off the dirt,—
   - **(A) write the plant's name**
   - **(C) cut a specimen of the plant**
   - **(B) blot with paper towels**
   - **(D) fold the newspaper over**

3. Before folding over the newspaper,—
   - **(A) have all plant parts showing**
   - **(C) put the plant in a warm, dry room**
   - **(B) place the plant between heavy books**
   - **(D) wash off the dirt**

4. After you mount the specimen on a sheet of paper,—
   - **(A) arrange it on newspaper**
   - **(C) write its name and location**
   - **(B) take a photograph of it**
   - **(D) place it between books**

39

DIRECTIONS: To rise to the surface, use your arms and swim fins. Make sure you are looking up so that you can see the surface. When you get about six feet below the surface, stop for a second to see that there is no boat, dock, or other obstacle right above you. You can hear well underwater. Your ears may hear an oncoming motorboat that your eyes might not be able to see. If all seems clear, propel yourself upward until you break through the surface.

1. These directions show you how to—
    (A) **enter the water**
    (B) **dive**
    (C) **rise to the surface**
    (D) **spear fish**

2. Remember—
    (A) **to listen and look**
    (B) **to look only**
    (C) **that sound travels poorly through water**
    (D) **that there is nothing to worry about**

3. You should stop about—
    (A) **two feet below the surface**
    (B) **ten feet below the surface**
    (C) **eight feet below the surface**
    (D) **six feet below the surface**

4. Remember to use—
    (A) **your arms and fins**
    (B) **just your arms**
    (C) **a rope**
    (D) **just your fins**

DIRECTIONS: Brush and comb your hair to remove dust and tangles. Then wet it with warm water. Next, lather the hair with shampoo. Now, using your fingertips, rub the lather into your hair and scalp. After you have thoroughly massaged your scalp, rinse it. Put on more lather. Massage your scalp again. Rinse thoroughly with hot water. If your hair squeaks when you pull it, you know it is clean.

1. The purpose of this article is to teach you how to—
   (A) clean your scalp
   (B) rinse your hair
   (C) wash your hair
   (D) prevent dandruff

2. Right after you lather your hair,—
   (A) brush and comb it
   (B) rinse it
   (C) see if it squeaks
   (D) massage your scalp

3. Before you massage the second time,—
   (A) pull your hair
   (B) brush and comb your hair
   (C) rinse your hair
   (D) lather your hair

4. Before your hair can squeak, it must be—
   (A) clean
   (B) wet
   (C) lathered
   (D) massaged

41

DIRECTIONS: Have a supply of wood and tinder on hand before you begin your campfire. Use three sticks, each about a foot long, to form a triangle. Place a large handful of tinder, such as wood shavings, bark, or dry weed tops inside the triangle. Light the tinder. Add more tinder. Then keep on adding larger pieces of fast-burning wood for kindling, such as willow, pine, or spruce. Add one piece at a time. Don't make the fire larger than is necessary. When it is the right size, add slower-burning fuel, such as oak, hickory, or ash wood.

1. These directions show you how to—
   (A) **put out a fire**
   (B) **cook over a fire**
   (C) **protect the outdoors**
   (D) **make a campfire**

2. Hickory, ash, and oak—
   (A) **are never used**
   (B) **are added first**
   (C) **burn quickly**
   (D) **burn slowly**

3. The fire is formed in the shape of a—
   (A) **triangle**
   (B) **circle**
   (C) **square**
   (D) **crescent**

4. You first light the—
   (A) **kindling**
   (B) **triangle**
   (C) **tinder**
   (D) **oak, hickory, or ash**

DIRECTIONS: At first your skin will tingle and become red. Then it will turn pale gray or grayish yellow. You won't feel anything. Don't rub or use heating pads or snow on the frozen area. Don't expose it to a hot radiator, fire, or stove. Get indoors immediately. Warm the frozen area of skin as soon as you can by placing it in warm water, not above 100° Fahrenheit. Dry it off right away. Then cover the area with warm towels. Take a warm drink of tea, coffee, or beef broth.

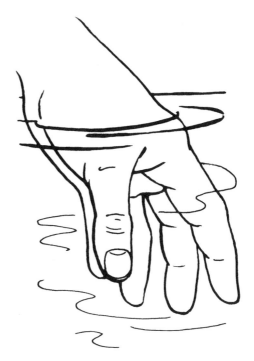

1. These directions tell how to—
   - (A) stay cool
   - (B) enjoy the out-of-doors
   - (C) treat frostbite
   - (D) fight the cold

2. Remember to—
   - (A) rub the area
   - (B) stay outdoors
   - (C) put snow on the area
   - (D) come indoors

3. The water used on the frozen skin should be—
   - (A) warm
   - (B) cool
   - (C) extremely cold
   - (D) extremely hot

4. Remember to—
   - (A) use no liquids
   - (B) sit close to the fire
   - (C) take a warm drink
   - (D) use heating pads

DIRECTIONS: Have your dog face you. Hold the leash in your right hand as you push down the dog's hindquarters with your left hand and say, "Sit." Always use the same command. Press down until the dog takes the proper sitting position. If your pet lies down, grasp the loose skin around its neck until it is sitting up. This won't hurt your dog. If the animal tries to get up when you remove your hand, push it down again and repeat the command. Reward your pet with praise when the order is followed promptly.

1. These directions show how to teach a dog to—
   - (A) stand
   - (B) shake hands
   - (C) beg
   - (D) sit

2. Grasp the skin around its neck—
   - (A) to pull it up
   - (B) until it barks
   - (C) to hold it down
   - (D) as a reward

3. Remember to—
   - (A) change the command
   - (B) give the same command
   - (C) hold the leash tightly
   - (D) stand behind your pet

4. When your pet sits, it is important to—
   - (A) say nothing
   - (B) praise the animal
   - (C) try another trick
   - (D) show off your dog

DIRECTIONS: Here is how to find someone's pulse rate (the number of heartbeats) per minute. The patient's arm should be resting in a comfortable position. Put the tips of your first three fingers (not your thumb) on the inside of the wrist just below the patient's thumb. Locate the pulse. When you can plainly feel it, look at the second hand of your watch. Count the beats for thirty seconds and multiply by two. This will give you the pulse rate per minute.

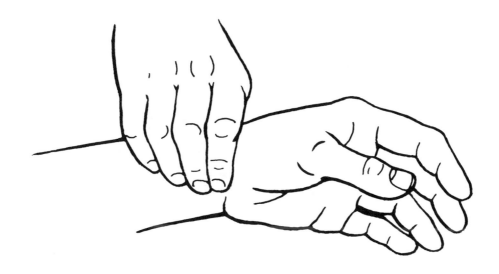

1. These directions show you how to—
    (A) **give first aid**   (B) **tell time**
    (C) **take a person's pulse**   (D) **take a person's temperature**

2. You will need a watch with—
    (A) **large numbers**   (B) **an hour hand**
    (C) **a second hand**   (D) **a leather band**

3. You should count the beats for—
    (A) **one minute**   (B) **two minutes**
    (C) **thirty seconds**   (D) **one hour**

4. You must use your—
    (A) **thumb**   (B) **first three fingers**
    (C) **first two fingers**   (D) **whole hand**

DIRECTIONS: Once your dog knows how to "sit up" and "speak," it is ready to learn how to beg. To do this trick, first get your pet in a sitting position. As you say the word *beg*, raise the animal by its front legs. Make sure the chin is held high. Hold a treat a few inches above its head. When your pet barks, give it both a treat and praise. Keep repeating this trick until your dog sits up without any assistance and barks immediately at the command to beg.

1. These directions show how to train a dog to—
   (A) shake hands
   (B) fetch
   (C) roll over
   (D) beg

2. The dog must —
   (A) say, "Thank you"
   (B) jump all over you
   (C) hold its chin up
   (D) wag its tail

3. The dog is rewarded with—
   (A) a treat only
   (B) praise only
   (C) a pat
   (D) a treat and praise

4. When you say, "Beg," your dog must—
   (A) sit up and bark
   (B) be silent
   (C) move slowly
   (D) wag its tail

DIRECTIONS: If a blister appears on your skin, wash the area with soap and water. Dry it carefully. Then cover it with an adhesive bandage. If the blister looks as if it might break, it should be punctured and drained. If a doctor is not available to do this, it should be done by an adult. The procedure is as follows. Use a needle that has been sterilized. Push the needle through the skin at the side of the blister. Then insert it up higher into the blister. Gently press out the liquid. Then cover the blister with a clean new bandage.

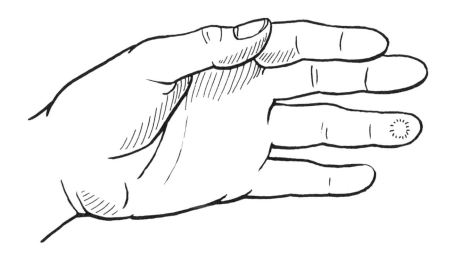

---

1. From this article you will learn how to—
   - **(A) bandage a wound**
   - **(B) sterilize a needle**
   - **(C) care for a blister**
   - **(D) treat an open wound**

2. Right after the blister is punctured,—
   - **(A) cover it with a bandage**
   - **(B) let it dry**
   - **(C) remove the liquid**
   - **(D) wash it**

3. If it looks as if the blister will break,—
   - **(A) lift it off**
   - **(B) rub it**
   - **(C) puncture it**
   - **(D) put medicine on it**

4. Before the liquid is pressed out,—
   - **(A) stroke the blister**
   - **(B) insert the needle into the side**
   - **(C) cover it with a clean bandage**
   - **(D) dry the area**

A. Exercising Your Skill

There are different kinds of **directions**. Some directions are the kind you see in workbooks and on tests. Some directions tell you how to do or make something. Others tell you how to carry out an experiment.

Read these sets of directions. Think about what the directions tell you to do. Match each set of directions with a title from the box. Write the numbers 1, 2, 3, and 4 on your paper. Next to each number, write the title that fits the directions.

Experiment Directions	Workbook Directions
Game Directions	How-To Directions

1. To play tic-tac-toe, draw a grid of two line across and two lines down to make nine spaces. Two players take turns making X's and O's in spaces. The first one to get three X's or O's in a line is the winner.
2. First, magnetize a needle by stroking it with a strong bar magnet. Always stroke in the same direction. Then shove the needle through a cork. Float the cork in water. Does the needle always point the same way?
3. Listen to the final sound in the word your teacher says. Write down the word. Circle the letter that stands for the final sound.
4. You can make a stringed instrument with a book, a paper cup, and a rubber band. Place the paper cup on the book, close to one end, with the open end of the cup up. Stretch the rubber band the long way around the book and over the cup. Strum the rubber band over the cup. Then strum the stretched part on each side of the cup. Do you hear three different sounds?

B. Expanding Your Skill

Discuss the different kinds of directions with your classmates. Answer the following questions.

- How are all directions the same? How are they different?
- What kinds of directions list materials?
- What kinds of directions usually have illustrations?

C. Exploring Language

The following things can help make directions clear.

- a title
- a list of materials at the beginning
- steps that are numbered or time-order words
- illustrations

Choose one of the sets of directions in Part A. On your paper, rewrite the directions to make them clearer. If materials are used, list them first. Number the steps or use time-order words to show the order to follow. Add illustrations if you think they will help. Give the directions a title.

D. Expressing Yourself

Choose one of these activities.

1. Prepare illustrated directions for an everyday situation, such as using a coin-operated vending machine, making a sandwich, or borrowing a book from the school or local library. As you write your directions, think about how you can make them clear and easy to follow.

2. Follow the directions for one of the experiments in this book. Explain your results to the class.

3. Prepare a demonstration speech for your class. First decide on something that you know how to make or do. Then gather the materials you will need to make or do it. Write directions that tell what to do. Make sure they are in the right order. Then practice your speech. When you give a demonstration speech, you explain what to do while you actually follow the directions yourself. Practicing in front of a mirror is a good idea. When you feel ready, teach the class how to do or make something by explaining it and showing it at the same time.

DIRECTIONS: If there's a fishhook embedded in your skin, get a doctor. If it is in the finger or arm (don't touch it if it's in the face) and no doctor is available, take these steps. Push the hook until the barbed end comes all the way through the skin. Don't pull it back out, or the flesh will tear. Cut off the barbed end with clippers or pliers. Then pull out the hook. Wash the area with soap and water. Cover with a bandage. See a doctor as soon as you can.

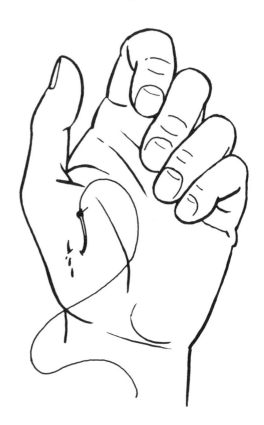

1. These directions show you how to—
   (A) **bait a hook**
   (B) **fish**
   (C) **remove a fishhook**
   (D) **get hooked**

2. The barbed end of the fishhook should be—
   (A) **pushed through the skin**
   (B) **pushed halfway through the skin**
   (C) **pushed out the gill**
   (D) **washed carefully**

3. Don't pull the hook out until the—
   (A) **barbed end is cut**
   (B) **barb gets deeper**
   (C) **skin is washed**
   (D) **barb gets rusty**

4. If the hook is stuck in your face,—
   (A) **keep pulling**
   (B) **try another sport**
   (C) **twist it**
   (D) **don't touch it**

DIRECTIONS: Here is a good way to arrange the clothes in your closet. Put the clothes that you don't wear often in a part of the closet that is hard to reach. Put the clothes that you use every day in an easy-to-reach part of the closet. Put shoes on racks or in shoe bags that can be hung on the inside of the closet door. Be sure to remove any clothes that you never use.

1. From these directions you learn how to—
   (A) **keep your clothes clean** (B) **dress properly**
   (C) **organize your clothes closet** (D) **remove all furnishings**

2. The clothes you wear frequently go—
   (A) **in an easy-to-reach spot** (B) **outside the closet door**
   (C) **in boxes on shelves** (D) **on the floor**

3. The inside of the closet door is a good place for—
   (A) **shoe bags** (B) **hat boxes**
   (C) **clothes chutes** (D) **heavy baggage**

4. It is important to remove clothes that are never—
   (A) **borrowed** (B) **wrinkled**
   (C) **taxed** (D) **worn**

DIRECTIONS: Get the person to blink his or her eyes. The tears may help wash the cinder from the eye. If the cinder is under the upper eyelid, pull the upper lid down and out. The edge of the lower lid may brush away the cinder. If the cinder is under the lower lid, pull the lower lid down gently and remove the cinder with the end of a clean, damp handkerchief. If you aren't successful or if the cinder isn't on the white part of the eye, see a doctor immediately.

1. These directions tell you how to—
    (A) care for the sick
    (B) bathe the eye
    (C) get something out of the eye
    (D) see better

2. Remove the cinder with—
    (A) your thumb
    (B) a dirty cloth
    (C) a handkerchief
    (D) a cotton ball

3. To get a cinder from under the upper eyelid,—
    (A) pull the upper lid up
    (B) blink a few times
    (C) rub the lid as hard as you can
    (D) pull the upper lid down and out

4. If you aren't successful,—
    (A) never stop trying
    (B) let all your friends try
    (C) tell the patient to use the other eye
    (D) see a doctor

DIRECTIONS: Crash! Bang! Boom! Sound travels about a mile in five seconds. Light travels much more quickly. When you see a flash of lightning during a storm, begin to count. Count slowly, saying one-one thousand, two-one thousand, and so on. Count until you hear the thunder that goes with the lightning strike. If you reached five, the lightning and the storm are one mile away. If you reached ten, they are two miles away.

1. These directions tell you how to—
   - (A) **keep safe during a storm**
   - (B) **count to several thousand**
   - (C) **figure a storm's distance**
   - (D) **count lightning flashes**

2. This activity is based on the fact that—
   - (A) **lightning often strikes trees**
   - (B) **many people count too fast**
   - (C) **light travels faster than sound**
   - (D) **some storms travel slowly**

3. This means that a watcher—
   - (A) **sees the lightning first**
   - (B) **hears the thunder first**
   - (C) **counts only during the thunder**
   - (D) **only counts to ten**

4. A count of ten means the lightning and storm are—
   - (A) **one mile away**
   - (B) **passing overhead**
   - (C) **two miles away**
   - (D) **moving away from you**

DIRECTIONS: Ask a volunteer to think of a number and then to whisper it to each member of the group. Tell the volunteer not to let you hear it. Then ask the person to multiply that number by 5 and add 2. Multiply the total by 4. Then add 3. Next, multiply by 5. Finally, ask the volunteer to add 7 and give you the result. Ignore the two figures on the right and you have the answer. The remaining number is the one the volunteer was thinking of.

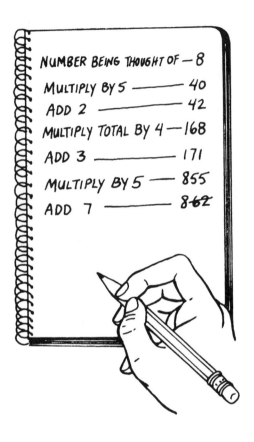

NUMBER BEING THOUGHT OF — 8
MULTIPLY BY 5 ———— 40
ADD 2 ———— 42
MULTIPLY TOTAL BY 4 — 168
ADD 3 ———— 171
MULTIPLY BY 5 — 855
ADD 7 ———— 862

1. If you follow these directions, you will—
   (A) **become better at arithmetic**   (B) **be able to guess numbers**
   (C) **be able to read minds**   (D) **become an entertainer**

2. First, the volunteer must—
   (A) **multiply by 5**   (B) **add 2**
   (C) **whisper to others**   (D) **think of a number**

3. To do this trick correctly, you must be able to—
   (A) **write on a chalkboard**   (B) **write with chalk**
   (C) **do math problems quickly**   (D) **use an adding machine**

4. At first, the number is known only by the—
   (A) **person performing the trick**   (B) **members of the group**
   (C) **volunteer**   (D) **teacher**

DIRECTIONS: When you carry a large object up or down the stairs, make sure that your vision isn't blocked. Vision helps you maintain balance. There's no rush either. You should keep one hand free to grasp the railing should you start to stumble. If the object can't be carried with only one arm, get help. If help isn't available, put the package on the steps, and move it up or down one step at a time. If the load can be divided, make two or three trips.

1. These directions show you how to—
   - (A) **carry objects that are small**
   - (B) **strengthen your muscles**
   - (C) **carry objects up and down stairs**
   - (D) **become a weight lifter**

2. Don't forget to keep—
   - (A) **both hands on the rail**
   - (B) **both hands on the object**
   - (C) **one hand free**
   - (D) **both hands free**

3. Remember to—
   - (A) **accept no help**
   - (B) **carry as much as possible**
   - (C) **rush**
   - (D) **divide the load, if possible**

4. There's nothing wrong with—
   - (A) **moving it up or down one step at a time**
   - (B) **closing your eyes**
   - (C) **taking two steps at a time**
   - (D) **throwing the package down to a friend below**

DIRECTIONS: Look in the direction you want the horse to go, not at yourself or the horse. Keep holding the reins in both hands, and keep both hands close together. To turn to the right, pull the right hand slightly back toward your body. This puts a gentle, steady pressure on the right side of the horse's mouth, which will encourage it to move to the right. Press your left leg lightly against the horse's side. At the same time, press the left rein against the horse's neck.

1. These directions show you how to make a horse—
    (A) gallop   (B) halt
    (C) back up   (D) turn

2. Your hands should be—
    (A) on the saddle   (B) far apart
    (C) close together   (D) around the horse's neck

3. The reins must be—
    (A) held in both hands (B) yanked hard
    (C) held in one hand   (D) dropped

4. You must remember to look—
    (A) at the reins   (B) in the direction you want to go
    (C) at the horse   (D) at yourself

DIRECTIONS: Place the fish on a cutting board. Cut down just behind the gills until the knife strikes the backbone. Then twist the knife and cut along the backbone to the tail. Cut through the ribs and lift off the side of the fish in one piece. Turn the fish over and repeat this same procedure. Next, place each piece flesh-side down. Insert the knife between the skin and flesh, starting at the tail. Use a sawing motion to remove the skin. Then cut the rib bones free and discard them.

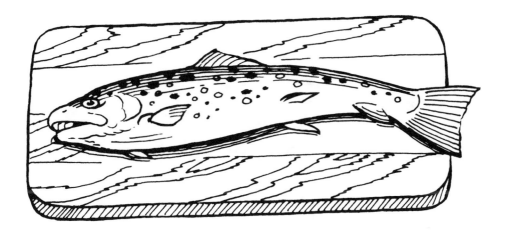

1. From these directions you should be able to—
   (A) remove a fish's bones   (B) catch a fish
   (C) hold a fish fry   (D) cook a fish

2. Just before you twist the knife,—
   (A) cut down behind the gills   (B) cut down to the tail
   (C) cut along the backbone   (D) lay the fish on the board

3. After you lift off the first side of the fish,—
   (A) turn the fish over   (B) skin the fish
   (C) cut the ribs   (D) clean the fish

4. Just before you cut the rib bones free,—
   (A) lift off the backbone   (B) skin the fish
   (C) place the flesh side   (D) cut behind the gills
       of the fish down

DIRECTIONS: You can remove a splinter if it is near the surface of the skin. See a doctor if it is deeply imbedded or very large. First, sterilize a needle and tweezers. Hold them in a flame for a few seconds. When the needle is cool, press it against the skin near the point of the splinter. Push the splinter toward the place where it entered. Use the tweezers to grasp the loosened end. Use soap and water to wash the area. Cover with a bandage.

1. These directions tell you how to—
    (A) treat a burn   **(B) remove a splinter**
    (C) treat a cut   **(D) stop a nosebleed**

2. Push the splinter—
    (A) right along   **(B) in deeper**
    (C) in the direction it is heading   **(D) in the direction it entered**

3. If the splinter is deeply imbedded,—
    (A) remove it yourself   **(B) ignore it**
    (C) call a doctor   **(D) cover it with a bandage**

4. To sterilize the needle and tweezers,—
    (A) hold them in a flame   **(B) wash them**
    (C) rub them with a cloth   **(D) put them in water**

UNIT 48

DIRECTIONS: Since you're sure to have some spills, it is important that you learn how to fall. Always try to fall in a sitting position. This is the most important thing to remember because then there is less chance of a serious injury. If you bend your knees, you'll be closer to the ice when you hit and the jolt will be less. Don't use your hands to break your fall. Not only are you likely to wind up with broken fingers or a broken arm, but you won't end up in a sitting position.

1. This article was written to show you how to—
   (A) maintain balance   (B) fall properly
   (C) prevent falling   (D) skate in a circle

2. Remember—
   (A) to grab a friend   (B) to use your hands
   (C) not to use your hands   (D) yell for help

3. Always try to fall—
   (A) headfirst   (B) on your arms
   (C) in a sitting position   (D) on your side

4. By bending your knees, you'll have—
   (A) no broken fingers   (B) more fun
   (C) less of a jolt   (D) a harder fall

DIRECTIONS: You can prevent insects from biting you. Before an outing, swim in a pool that has been chlorine-treated, or add a capful of chlorine bleach to your bath. Insects do not like the smell of chlorine or commercial insect repellents. They do like the way perfumed soaps and shampoos smell. The odor of perspiration also appeals to them. So keep your skin free of fragrances and as dry as possible. Don't eat peanuts or bananas before an outing. They both contain a substance (serotonin) that attracts mosquitoes. Keeping your skin covered as much as possible is one of the best ways of making sure you won't be bitten.

1. These directions tell you how to—
   - **(A) use chlorine**
   - **(B) prevent insect bites**
   - **(C) eat before an outing**
   - **(D) buy insect repellents**

2. The smells of soaps, shampoos, and body sweat—
   - **(A) stun bees**
   - **(B) scare away bugs**
   - **(C) kill mosquitoes**
   - **(D) attract insects**

3. Peanuts and bananas contain—
   - **(A) serotonin**
   - **(B) carotin**
   - **(C) plasma**
   - **(D) turpentine**

4. One of the best ways to keep bugs from biting is to—
   - **(A) sit in the sun**
   - **(B) carry an umbrella**
   - **(C) use perfumed soap**
   - **(D) cover your skin**

DIRECTIONS: Make sure everyone is accounted for. Leave a place for everyone to hold onto the boat. If life preservers are on board, grab them and put them on. If any lines are within reach, fasten everyone to the boat. Signal with whatever you have—a flag, shirt, bell, or horn. Stay calm. The most important thing to remember when your boat has overturned is to stay with the boat. Don't try to swim to shore. It may be farther away than it looks.

1. These directions tell you what to do when—
   - (A) out rowing
   - (B) out swimming
   - (C) your boat has overturned
   - (D) the motor stops

2. The most important thing to remember is to—
   - (A) row as fast as you can
   - (B) swim to shore
   - (C) practice swimming
   - (D) stay with the boat

3. The shore is always—
   - (A) close
   - (B) the same distance away
   - (C) many miles away
   - (D) farther away than it looks

4. The very first thing to do is—
   - (A) swim as fast as you can
   - (B) bail the boat out
   - (C) account for everybody
   - (D) start paddling

A. Exercising Your Skill

Sometimes illustrations can make directions clearer. Read these directions for making a paper jet plane.

1. Take an 8½ x 11-inch sheet of paper and fold it in half lengthwise.
2. Open out the paper and fold the two top corners down to the crease.
3. Fold the side corners down to the crease again.
4. Fold the two sides together along the original crease.
5. Fold each side back to the center crease line.
6. Hold the center fold, and straighten out the two sides so that it looks like a jet plane.
7. Put a small piece of tape on top of the jet in the middle to hold it together.
8. Draw decorations on the plane.
9. Write the plane's name on the side of the plane.

Which steps would be clearer with illustrations? Draw pictures to make the directions clearer.

B. Expanding Your Skill

Read this list of topics. Talk the topics over with your classmates. Decide which topics could best be explained if illustrations were included with the written steps. Explain why you think so.

How to Eat Spaghetti	How to Do a Magic Trick
How to Mark an Answer	How to Feed Tropical Fish
How to Tie-Dye a Shirt	How to Make Shadow Pictures
How to Use Sign Language	How to Play Musical Chairs

C. Exploring Language

The directions below are not very good. They contain information that is not needed. They don't list the materials you need. The steps are not in order, and there are no signal words to help make the order clear. Directions should not sound like a story. They should tell the reader what to do. Improve and rewrite the directions. Add illustrations to make the directions clearer.

> Once, I was playing with an old sock. I put it on my hand and pretended it was a ghost. All of a sudden, I realized I was using the sock like a puppet. So I decided to make some real sock puppets! I drew faces on the socks with felt-tipped markers. First, of course, I had to ask my mother for some old socks to use. I got some thread and cotton and pieces of fabric, and I cut out four pieces in the shape of a rabbit's ears. I got a needle and sewed two of the ear pieces together with a hole at the bottom. I sewed the ear together after I stuffed it with cotton. I did the same thing to make another ear. I sewed the ears on the puppet. I had a good time doing this, and I hope you will, too.

D. Expressing Yourself

Choose one of these activities.

1. Write a paragraph telling how to do one of the following. Remember to list the materials you will need, if any. Use time-order words to show the order of the steps.

   1. load a camera
   2. make a sandwich
   3. cure hiccups
   4. use chopsticks
   5. make a candle
   6. braid hair

2. Think about something you know how to do very well. Write directions for doing this thing. You may want to draw pictures to go along with your directions. Give your directions to a classmate. See whether your classmate can follow the directions.